Photos

Photos by Steven Townsend

Photos of Bear Mountain, New York; Vermont; Washington, DC; and others

All photos copyright Steven Townsend

Bear

Mountain

Rowboat on Hessian Lake

Upside Down

Autumn Leaves on Hessian Lake

Autumn Leaves

Lulu

Pine Tree

Pine Branches

Tree Roots

Tree Roots

Mount

Vernon

Barrels

Buckets

Hooks

Tree Roots

Tree Trunk

Spinning Wheels

Kenilworth Gardens

Broken Branch

Tree Trunk

Tree Trunk

Tree Trunk

Lily Pond

Lotus

Lotus

Lotus

Lotus

Lotus

Lotus

Water lily

Lotus and Moth

Vermont

Barber, Stowe Vermont

Scarecrow, Stowe Vermont

Autumn Leaves

Wooden Fence

Tree

Trees

Trees

Trees

Hills

The Valley

National Botanic Garden

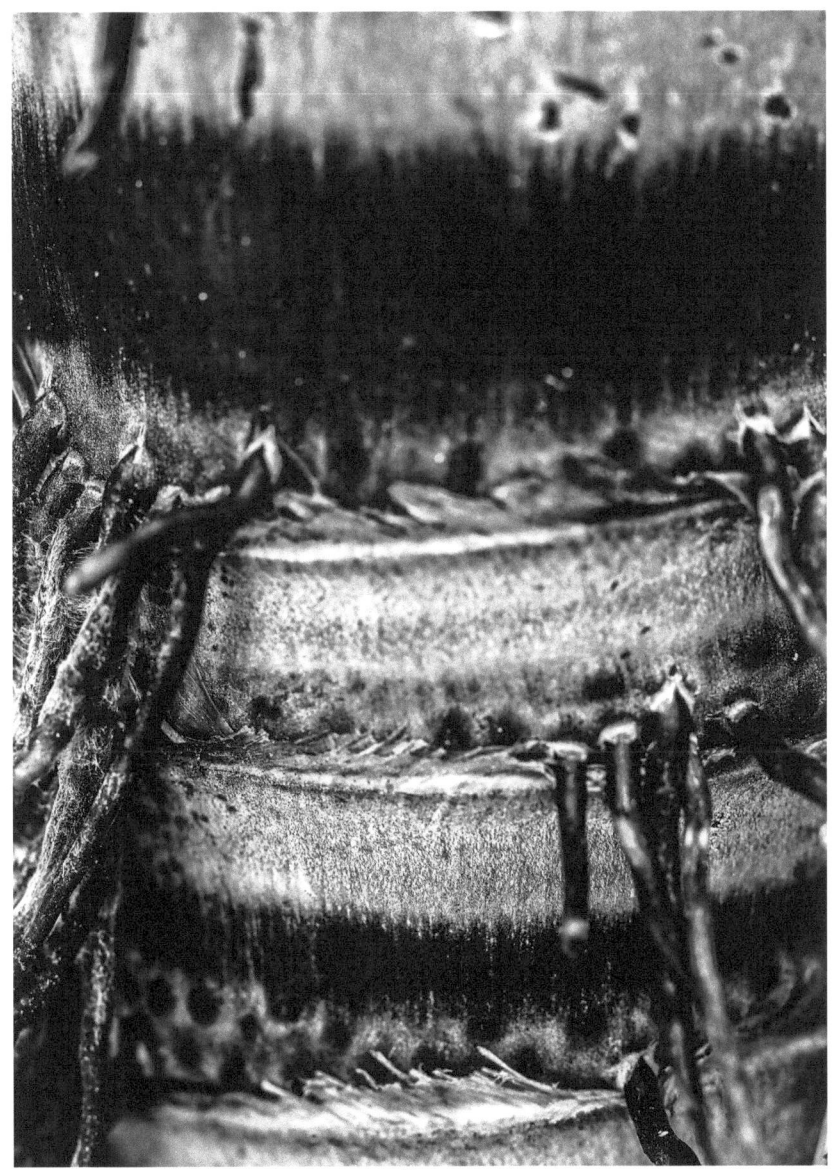

Abstract

Cactus Flower

Fruit

Leaf

Leaves

Leaves

Succulent

SW DC Arts Festival

Bass Player

Guitar Player

Sax Player

Bass Player and Singer

Colors

Death Valley and Northern California

Bush

Reeds

Sunrise, Death Valley

Tree, Napa California

Jellyfish, Monterey Aquarium

Fish, Monterey Aquarium

Fish, Monterey Aquarium

Other

Photos

Frank

Boxcar

www.ingramcontent.com/pod-product-compliance
Lightning Source LLC
Chambersburg PA
CBHW050748180526
45159CB00003B/1387